AMERICAN STEAM LOCOMOTIVES

Alive and still working today

Photography by Henry Rasmussen

Motorbooks International
Publishers & Wholesalers Inc.
Osceola, Wisconsin 54020, USA ®

First published in 1988 by Motorbooks
International Publishers & Wholesalers Inc,
P O Box 2, 729 Prospect Avenue, Osceola, WI
54020 USA

Printed and bound in Hong Kong

The information in this book is true and
complete to the best of our knowledge. All
recommendations are made without any
guarantee on the part of the author or
publisher, who also disclaim any liability
incurred in connection with the use of this
data or specific details.

**Library of Congress
Cataloging-in-Publication Data**
Rasmussen, Henry
  American steam locomotives.

  1. Locomotives—United States. I. Title.
TJ603.2.R37 1988 625.2'61'0973 87-31460
ISBN 0-87938-284-8

Motorbooks International books are also
available at discounts in bulk quantity for
industrial or sales-promotional use. For
details write to Special Sales Manager at the
Publisher's address

On the front cover: *Yosemite Mtn &
Sugar Pine Rail Road's engine 15 emerges
from its shed for work. The unit is a Shay
with its peculiar lopsided look.* **Back
cover:** *Engine 90, a Decapod-type Baldwin
employed by the Strasburg Rail Road,
Pennsylvania, waits impatiently while one
of its fifty-six-inch whitewalls gets a once-
over.* **Frontispiece:** *Engine 630, a
Consolidation-type Alco operated by the
Tennessee Valley Railroad Museum,
accelerates down the final straightaway
leading to the East Chattanooga depot.*
Title page: *A panoramic view shows the
Cumbres & Toltec train traversing the 175-
foot Los Pinos pile trestle.* **Contents
page:** *Engine 7002, an Atlantic-type
locomotive built by Pennsylvania Railroad's
Juniata shops, forms a blurry backdrop to
a collection of warning signs along the
Strasburg line.* **Page seven:** *Strasburg
Rail Road's engine 1223, an American-type
locomotive also built at the Juniata shops,
peers out at a passing train from its stall in
the enginehouse.* **Last page:** *A Cumbres &
Toltec train leaves behind a peaceful
picture of the earliest rider of the high
plains, the cowboy.*

Contents

Childhood Memories of Locomotives Missed

Introduction to Intrigue

A long time has passed since my childhood encounter with steam locomotives. Unfortunately, my contact with the black monsters was quite superficial; now I regret not having become more involved.

It was in the late-forties, and every morning I had to take the train to school. Of course, I remember the odor of smoke, streaming through the open windows in the spring like the sweet smell of adventure. And I remember the sound of the moaning and puffing and blowing of steam, accompanying the boarding of the passengers like the musical score of a movie. And I remember that sudden dunk from the first effort of the cylinders, and that staccato during acceleration, and that flattening-out as the locomotive reached operating speed.

But I never took the time to visit the roundhouse for a closer look. And I never asked the engineer for a ride in the cab; I don't even remember the wheel arrangement of these locomotives. And, of course, the investigation of such things as class, type, manufacturer, was never contemplated.

Now, forty years later, in the process of making this book and having spent a summer with steam locomotives, I have naturally had the strange experience of déjà vu. But this time, the gathering of facts, necessary for the text, forced me into a closer involvement, for which I'm grateful.

I have discovered that—to a larger degree, I believe, than in any other enthusiast field—the railroad fan is an avid photographer. For the benefit of just such an enthusiast, I will give some photographic notes.

I used only one camera: a 1974 vintage Mamiya RB67; heavy, but blessed with the capacity of taking large-format frames, 2¼ by 2¾ inches in size. I used three lenses: a 50 mm wide angle, a 90 mm normal and a 180 mm telephoto. I used no flash, and no filters, but occasionally a tripod. I used, as always, Kodak Ektachrome Professional 120 film, the 100 ASA color reversal version.

My status as a layman in the field of railroading is obvious, as the professional railroad fan will soon discover from the text. But perhaps this failing can be balanced by the photographs, for after all this book is a celebration of the visual intrigue of live steam.

As such, I hope, and suspect, it will bring back memories such as mine—pleasantly filled with nostalgia—of childhood locomotives missed.

A Name that Spanned the Era of Steam

Baldwin Locomotive Works

To have caused the creation of 1,500 locomotives would seem a most satisfying feat, an accomplishment to look back on with pride at the end of a long life. If Matthias Baldwin indeed contemplated this fact on his deathbed, he would certainly have felt even more satisfied had he been able to look into the future—the company he founded went on to become one of the world's largest manufacturers in the field. By the end of the era, the Baldwin Locomotive Works had built no less than 75,000 units.

But the road to success was less than smooth. Baldwin's first effort, Old Ironsides—delivered to the Philadelphia, Germantown and Norristown Railroad in 1832—was found wanting in important areas, and Baldwin never received payment in full. A few years later, the industry was ravaged by recession. Many of Baldwin's competitors folded. But, thanks to a creative arrangement with his creditors, he managed to stay in business, although shouldered with a debt burden that severely hampered the pace of his progress.

In 1842, the year Baldwin celebrated his tenth anniversary, only fourteen units were built. Not until 1846, which saw the completion of forty-two locomotives, would Baldwin again reach the volume of his earliest years. The company would be well past its twentieth anniversary before annual production reached sixty. Finally in 1865, the year preceding Matthias Baldwin's death, 115 units were built. Success now seemed inevitable.

Indeed, by the turn of the century, Baldwin had become a household name in America—and around the globe. To read the record of export destinations is to take a journey to the most exotic corners of the world: Peru, Madagascar, Sumatra . . . the list is as long as the road to Manchuria.

World War I brought expansion of hitherto unknown proportions; 1918 saw 3,580 units roll off the line. In 1923, rich with profits from this bonanza, Baldwin employed 21,500 workers, and its main plant, located in Eddystone—a suburb of Philadelphia, Pennsylvania—consisted of a sprawling complex occupying 616 acres on the shore of the Delaware River.

In the thirties, the demise of steam became inevitable. But, as with all death struggles, a final burst was still to come, brought on by World War II. Then, in 1956, came the bitter end. By that time the company had become part of an industrial conglomerate, and the spirit of the pioneer locomotive builder gradually dissolved into a host of diversified endeavors.

Magnificent Baldwins Show Their Mettle

In the picture on the previous page, photographed at Chama, New Mexico, Cumbres & Toltec Scenic Rail Road's engine 489—a Mikado-type Baldwin—stands slumbering in the afternoon sun. Its vital signs, the breath of smoke from the stack and the puffs of steam from the cylinders, show that it is alive and well. The picture to the left catches another Baldwin napping. The Consolidation-type engine 40 enjoys a well-deserved pause, having just exhausted itself on the grades of the Georgetown Loop. Seen in the picture above, the classic Baldwin manufacturer's brass plate, here mounted on the smokebox door of East Broad Top Rail Road's Mikado-type engine 15. Seen on the next spread, Strasburg's Decapod-type Baldwin, engine 90, builds up steam for the return run to the East Strasburg depot.

Builder of Corporate Clout and Big Boys

American Locomotive Company

The failure of the firm's first locomotive led to a false beginning which almost caused the company to miss the train. The year was 1848, the place was Schenectady, New York. A group of businessmen with John Ellis acting as a front, managed to raise the $50,000 required to entice the Norris brothers—the famous locomotive builders—to set up shop in the area. Their first creation was named Lightning. It was indeed fast, although too heavy for the track. Worse yet, it did not generate any orders. The Norris brothers were sent packing, and the plant was sold to pay the taxes.

But Ellis and his colleagues had not lost faith in the basic soundness of the locomotive business. By 1851, under the name Schenectady Locomotive Works, they were back in action. This effort might also have failed, however, had it not been for another famous builder, Walter McQueen. Under his leadership, the next few years saw the completion of more than 200 locomotives.

A few years later, thanks to deft maneuvering during the financial panic of 1857, Ellis managed to obtain majority control of the company. Luckily, the decade following turned out to be a period of booming business, largely as a result of orders stemming from the Civil War. This era also saw the company create one of railroad history's legends, the Jupiter, a veteran of the Promontory Point festivities that celebrated the completion of the transcontinental railroad.

Toward the end of the century, another famous engineer, A. J. Pitkin, joined the firm. Under his direction, several notable designs were created, among them the high-speed 4-4-0 of the New York Central & Hudson River Rail Road. Pitkin subsequently advanced to the top management spot. From this position he led the company into the new century, and on to the formation, in 1901, of the American Locomotive Company, a conglomerate of six locomotive builders. In time this organization, from 1955 on known as Alco, would become one of the world's largest locomotive manufacturers.

In the twenties, twenty-five percent of Alco's production consisted of electric locomotives, and later, after World War II, seventy-five percent of the capacity was taken up by diesel manufacture. A last hurrah for steam came during the war. It was the legendary Big Boy, one of the largest types of locomotives ever built. Alco hung on for another couple of decades, until in 1968 the doors of the old Schenectady plant closed for good.

Alco Epitomizes Heavy Metal Appeal

Many enthusiasts feel that Alco built some of the best-looking locomotives in the business. The picture on the previous page and the one on the following double spread—both featuring the same Ten-Wheeler-type 1907 Alco—certainly give credence to their contention. North Freedom's engine 1385 was photographed first as its massive countenance—floating on a cloud of steam—approaches the corner of the engine house, then as it pulls up parallel with the building, showing off that classically purposeful silhouette. Seen on this page, a view from inside the cab. Standing out among the clutter of plumbing is, on the right—the engineer's side—the long, horizontal throttle lever. The short, horizontal lever operates the main brake reservoir. Behind it, a similar lever operates a separate brake reservoir for the locomotive only. To the far right, by the window, the vertical reverse gear lever.

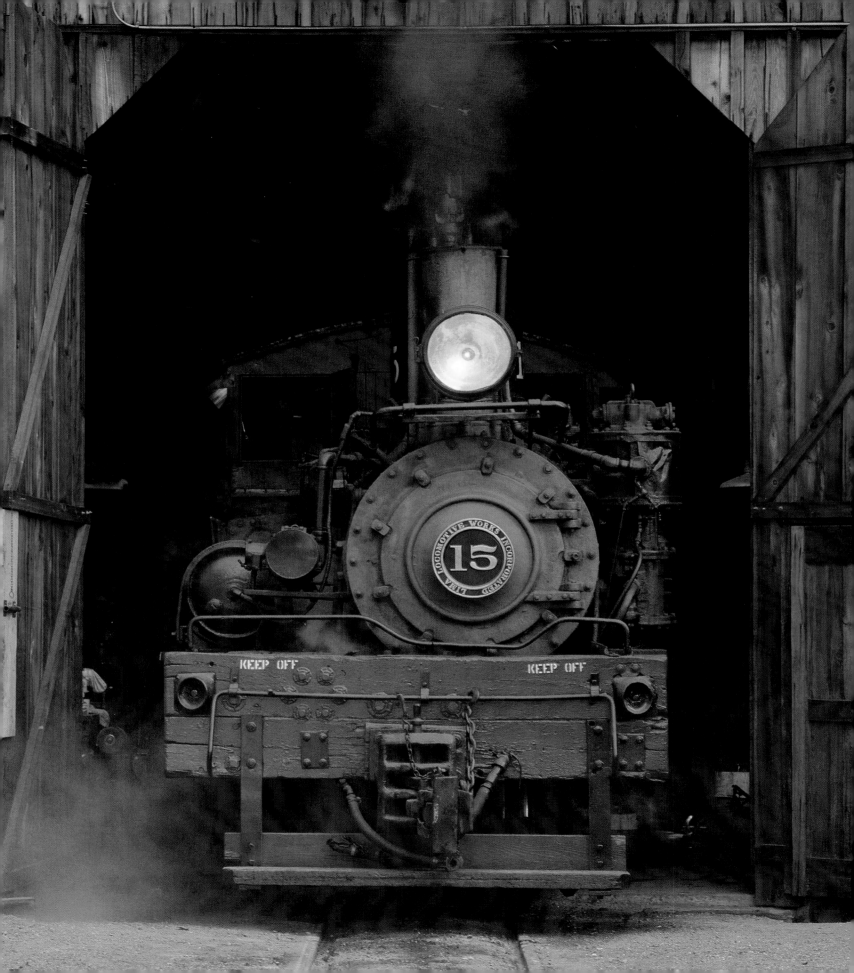

Uniquely Geared Toward the Logging Trade

Lima Locomotive Works

Ephraim Shay was a man of many talents. Born in Sherman, Ohio, he received his education in New Jersey, ultimately putting himself through medical school by teaching on the side. The Civil War saw him in the Union Army Corps of Engineers. When hostilities ended, he began practicing medicine in Norwalk, Ohio. Apparently not satisfied with this vocation, the early-1870s found him executing an abrupt career change; after a move to Haring, Michigan, he ventured into the lumber business.

The experience of several nearly snowless winters, a condition causing serious transportation problems for the loggers in the region, prompted Shay to devise a method of hauling logs by using horse-drawn cars rolling on wooden rails. Later, he constructed a crude locomotive, but the contraption proved to be hard on the track—curiously, much more so than the heavier cars. The solution, Shay concluded, was to fit the locomotive with the same wheel arrangement as used on the cars, thus equalizing load distribution.

With the assistance of a machinery firm in Lima, Ohio, Shay proceeded to construct a locomotive equipped with two four-wheel trucks. Power was conveyed from two vertically mounted cylinders via rods to a crank that drove a horizontal shaft, running parallel to the track. The shaft, in turn, worked on gears attached to each of the four wheels on that side.

Shay spent the next five winters refining his creation, and by 1880 the merits of the unique locomotive came to the attention of his colleagues. Their enthusiasm indicated that there might be a ready market for manufacturing. Shay insisted he was not in the business of building locomotives, however, and referred interested parties to the Lima firm. Encouraged by an ever increasing flow of orders, the company gradually concentrated its efforts on locomotive manufacture. In time, a new name, Lima Locomotive Works, reflected this devotion.

The Shay locomotive went on to revolutionize the logging industry, to the point of quickly attaining a cult-like status. The success eventually spawned the creation of other geared locomotives, such as the Climax and the Heisler. But more than the competition from these imitators, the era of the Shay—culminating in the twenties—was brought to an end by the combined effects of the Great Depression and the motorized truck. In all, 2,761 Shays were built, the last unit emerging from the shop in 1945.

A Maze of Moving Machinery

It's a cinch to separate a Shay from other locomotives. The frontal view on the previous page, snapped as Yosemite Mtn & Sugar Pine's engine 15 emerges from its shed, reveals the curiously lopsided look caused by the offset boiler. This was done to make room, as well as to provide counterbalance, for the cylinders placed on the opposite side. The Shay looks equally original in profile, as the series of three cylinders—seen in the picture to the right—makes for easy recognition. Above, the close-up focuses on one of the wheels and its gear mechanism, all kept turning smoothly with the aid of ample amounts of grease. On the following double spread, Illinois Railway Museum's engine 5 stands silhouetted against a smoky morning sky. This is an example of the famous Pacific Coast-type, available from 1927 and on—a much-improved design, built to compete with imitators muzzling in on the traditional Shay territory.

Mementos From the Era
of Mastodons

Main Line Excursion Excitement

Not only is it a sad reality, but also a surprising fact, that so little remains from the glory days of the steam era. A number of museums do display historic pieces; a limited few can be operated, however. These are occasionally steamed up for the benefit of railroad fans, but most stand in a state of frozen motion.

The number of steam locomotives still roaming freely in their natural habitat, according to a survey of the tourist-type establishments operating in the United States, totals approximately 200. Of these, about forty percent are Baldwins, fifteen percent Alcos, and ten percent Shays. The remaining thirty-five percent consists of products from a variety of manufacturers, and are primarily of a smaller type—for reasons of economical operation—such as Heislers, Climaxes and Porters.

Some of the causes of this regrettable state of affairs—referring now not to the operators of live-steam railroads, for they are certainly conveyors of enthusiasm and conservators of volunteer spirit but to the fact that so few steam locomotives have survived—are found in two age-old faults of the human race, ignorance and greed. Blame may also be aimed at a phenomenon

encountered by all championers of against-the-stream causes, corporate indifference.

The first collective catastrophe to hit the herd of steam locomotives came in the twenties, with the arrival of alternative power sources. Later, the general demise of the railroad as a mode of transportation, caused by the invasion of the truck and the automobile, raised further havoc. Thus, the moment of truth—that point when it became more profitable to scrap the old engine than to let it occupy space—always inevitably arrived.

The last decades of steam saw the emergence of the most impressive creations of all time. These were the streamlined giants, pulling trains with fancy names—the Daylight, the Twentieth Century Limited. And they were the ultimate mastodons—the Challengers, the Big Boys. Thanks to the farsightedness of two railroads in particular, the Union Pacific and the Norfolk Southern, some of these creations have been preserved, and can still occasionally be seen in action, regrettably only on a limited basis.

It may be a waste of emotion to hope and wait for a day when it would again be possible to watch a Big Boy make its way up the Wahsatch grade. But in the meantime, the sight of Norfolk Southern's 611 and 1218 provide ample consolation.

One Million Pounds, Plus Power to Match

Engine 611—seen, on the previous spread, working a grade near Roanoke, Virginia, and, to the right, resting at the Norfolk Southern's Roanoke depot—is the sole survivor of fourteen passenger locomotives constructed by Norfolk & Western's Roanoke shops between 1941 and 1950. The driving wheels of this 4-8-4 giant, stand seventy inches tall. Maximum tractive effort is 80,000 pounds, boiler pressure 300 pounds per square inch. Total weight is 872,000 pounds, overall length 109 feet. Another Roanoke-built survivor is the articulated 1218, above, a 2-6-6-4 freight locomotive, built in 1943. Tractive effort is 97,000 pounds, weight 952,000 pounds and length 121 feet. On the following spread, the fireman of engine 1218 is miniaturized by the massive size of the machinery.

28

Historic Route Offers Breathtaking Ride

Tennessee Valley Railroad Museum

The Tennessee Valley Railroad operates along a scenic route of historic significance. The original line, part of a system linking Charleston with Memphis, was laid out more than 130 years ago. Subsequent construction of the 986-foot Missionary Ridge tunnel, completed in 1858, finally provided rail access to Chattanooga.

In 1863, shortly after Sherman's troops had crossed the nearby Tennessee River, a group of Confederate soldiers penetrated the tunnel and mounted a surprise attack against the Yankees. This was one of the first skirmishes of the battle of Missionary Ridge. The battle was eventually won by the North and, in effect, sealed the fate of the Confederacy.

The tunnel took two years to build—considerably longer than called for by the plans—and the staggering cost of the undertaking ultimately forced the Chattanooga, Harrison, Georgetown & Charleston Railroad into bankruptcy. The line was subsequently purchased by the Eastern Tennessee & Georgia Railroad. Finally, in 1894, ownership was transferred to the Southern Railway which, in 1969, donated the original right-of-way, including the tunnel, to the Tennessee Valley Railroad Museum.

The origin of the museum can be traced to a group of railroad enthusiasts, who, inspired by the idea of building such an institution, began meeting in 1959. Formally chartered as a nonprofit educational organization in 1961, the group was able to forge ahead with specific plans. The next eight years were spent collecting equipment and searching for a suitable location. By 1969, museum volunteers were ready to begin reconstruction of the old line, starting with the East Chattanooga storage area. The next phase called for the laying of track. The effort was soon halted, however, by the need to build a bridge—a formidable task—finally completed in 1977.

Today, the East Chattanooga facility boasts both an engine restoration shop and a depot, as well as a turntable—originally from Macon, Georgia. A fine collection of passenger cars and locomotives, among them the last Baldwin built in 1956, is also housed here. At the other end of the three-mile track, reached after a breathtaking crossing of the Chickamauga Creek, the museum has built another depot, as well as a wye, a Y-shaped track allowing locomotives to maneuver themselves around to always face forward at the head of the train. Future plans include a connection with downtown Chattanooga and its famous Choo-Choo complex.

Fifty Feet Above
the Chickamauga Creek

On the previous spread, engine 630 and its tail of passenger cars makes the dramatic crossing of the Chickamauga Creek bridge, the most spectacular of the three bridges along the route. All bridges are in top condition and have had no speed limit constrictions imposed on them, thus the speed used on the rest of the track— between 20 and 25 miles per hour— is also kept when crossing the bridges. The Chickamauga bridge was completed in 1914. Parts of the span, which has a total length of 385 feet, came from other old railroad bridges in the area. An indication of the difference in component sizes resulting from this cost-saving measure can be seen in the picture on this spread. The fireman—silhouetted against a piece of sky between the cab and the tender—is about to send a shovel of coal into the firebox. From this vantage point, should he decide to look down, the fireman can catch a glimpse of the smooth waters of the Chickamauga, flowing fifty feet below.

The Sweet Smell of Billowing Smoke

The picture above, photographed from atop the smoke-engulfed tender, shows engine 630 as it winds its way through the lush Chattanooga vegetation. The picture to the right, photographed from a diesel switcher running just ahead of the Alco, captures the locomotive as the massive front splits the air like an iron fist.

Tied Up at Night, the Giant Naps

Tennessee Valley's Alco was built in 1903. It first served on the Southern system, where it hauled freight, but was later sold to the East Tennessee & Western North Carolina railroad. In 1967, it was returned to Southern and employed in its steam excursion program. The Alco, which came to Chattanooga in 1978, weighs 360,000 pounds with a tender that holds 12½ tons of coal and 8,000 gallons of water. Maximum tractive effort is 46,700 pounds at 200 psi of boiler pressure. Today, the old faithful—which is thought to have logged as many as four million miles—is seldom pushed above 180 psi. The picture on the previous spread shows the Alco tied up for the night. Preparations for the night's slumber include building a mound of coal in the middle of the grate. The smokestack is covered and the fire door closed, all to keep combustion to a minimum. The picture on this spread shows the innards of the napping giant, with smoke seeping gently through the holes in the fire door.

Rebirth of the Road to Paradise

Strasburg Rail Road

Chartered in 1832, the Strasburg Rail Road, located a short distance from Lancaster—right in the heart of Pennsylvania's Dutch Country—is the nation's oldest short-line railroad still in operation. While it is unclear exactly when the first wheels rolled on the rails, records show that the road was incorporated in 1851. Trains on the 4½-mile track transported both freight and passengers to the Leaman Place depot in Paradise, where the line connected with the Pennsylvania Railroad.

At the turn of the century, a streetcar operating between Lancaster and Strasburg diverted much of the passenger traffic, and the railroad had to be content to exist mainly on freight revenue. Over the decades, as freight hauling gradually turned into a chore for trucks, this source of income dwindled as well, until in 1957, the line—drowned both in red ink and flood waters from a torrential rain—was forced to cease operation.

In 1959, a group of enthusiasts managed to scrape together enough funds to purchase the line, which through the years of neglect, had all but vanished in a forest of weed and brush. But a valiant effort uncovered the track, and the first train of the new era could traverse the historic distance from Strasburg to Paradise.

At this point, the single passenger car was pulled by a small gasoline locomotive, the Plymouth, which was part of the purchase and had been bought new by the original owners in 1926. But it was soon realized that in order to attract a larger crowd, one simply had to have a steam locomotive; engine 31, a 1908 former Canadian 0-6-0 Baldwin, arrived in 1960, and the volume of passengers, as well as revenue, took an immediate jump.

The next item to arrive was an 1882 depot from East Petersburg, twenty miles away. It was moved in nine sections and reassembled on its new location and, of course, renamed East Strasburg. Next, a new engine house was built, and with this addition came room for further expansion in the locomotive department. The wheels of progress were in motion.

Today, the Strasburg Rail Road is one of the most successful steam operations in the country. Management runs an efficient tourist trade without sacrificing the enthusiasm that attracts the railroad fan. The appreciation of the latter is ensured by a collection of beautifully restored passenger cars and, most importantly, an outstanding stable of five operating steam locomotives.

Rolling Twenty Feet Per Revolution

The photographs on this and the previous page show engine 7002 at speed on the line, passing ripening corn fields and arriving at the depot, passing restored passenger cars. The 7002 is an Atlantic-type 4-4-2, built by the Pennsylvania Railroad's own shop in 1902. It was first numbered 8063, and was a sister of the original 7002, which, at the head of the Pennsylvania Special—in the course of making up time on the open stretches through Ohio—set a world steam locomotive speed record of 127 mph. With driving wheels measuring seventy-seven inches, each revolution sends the engine rolling twenty feet. Pictured on the following spread, pulling a line of passenger cars, is another classic, engine 90. The 1924 Baldwin is a Decapod-type 2-10-0, formerly of the Great Western Railway. The wheels measure fifty-six inches. Total weight is 371,500 pounds, including a tender that holds 18½ tons of coal and 8,500 gallons of water. Maximum tractive effort, at a boiler pressure of 200 psi, is 46,500 pounds.

In the Early Morning, the Engine Erupts

The morning is a time of opportunity for the railroad photographer. Not only is the light soft, but the maintenance procedures that occupy these early hours before the locomotive goes out on the line, offer spectacular possibilities. On this page, with the sun located behind the clouds of steam—the camera thus pointing into the light—Strasburg's 7002 looks as if it has just experienced a volcanic eruption. The hostler begins the morning by spreading out the coal in the firebox, goes on to clean the ash pan and dump the ashes, then rebuilds the fire, and as the pressure begins to rise—it is usually kept low during the night—he opens up the blow-cocks, which lets steam pass through the system, cleaning it from mineral build-ups and other pollutants. The picture on the following spread shows the result when the sun is behind the camera, which creates a softly lit view of the exquisite lines of this locomotive classic.

48

The Patina
of Passing Time

Although little exists of the original yard at Strasburg, the passing of time has lent a certain patina to the new buildings erected in the late-fifties and early-sixties, when the railroad was rebuilt after its reorganization. Thus, the yard of the resurrected Strasburg Rail Road, thanks to its heavy-duty traffic, its smoke, its grease, its coal—which all collaborate to quickly wear down any newness—has already, in its own right,

become something of a monument to railroading. A few casual sweeps with the camera brings into focus an old smokestack, to the left, leaning against a shack and looking somewhat misplaced without a boiler to adorn. And above, another picture appears in the viewfinder, a smokebox front assembly—including the door, but without the manufacturer's plate—lies abandoned beside the tracks. Corrosion, although a most regrettable phenomenon, has a way of creating decorative surfaces.

The Real Thing: Soot, Stains and All

East Broad Top Rail Road

The East Broad Top Rail Road is the oldest narrow-gauge line in the country, and the last—east of the Rocky Mountains—still in operation. Although the original charter was granted in 1856, the first stretch of track was not spiked until 1872. The road was built to haul coal from the East Broad Top mines of central Pennsylvania to the city of Mt. Union. Here, the narrow-gauge hoppers were re-trucked, instantly becoming fit for standard-gauge operation on the Pennsylvania Railroad.

With the hauling of coal remaining its main source of revenue, but income also being derived from the handling of general freight, express mail and passengers, the East Broad Top Rail Road managed to stay in business for more than eighty years.

In 1956, as engine 17 pulled into the yard for the last time, it was clear that operation had not come to an end due to lack of coal. Instead, the reason was that the market for this type of fuel had shrunk to the point where it was no longer economically feasible to work the mines. Thus was idled a facility which already in those days possessed the unspoiled character of a turn-of-the-century railroad.

When the line was sold to the Kovalchick Salvage Company only a few months after operation had ceased, it was commonly believed that the facility would be scrapped. There were even rumors to the effect that the railroad—lock, stock and locomotives—would be dismantled and moved to South America. When the line remained intact for several years, it was thought that the owner was only biding his time, waiting for scrap prices to rise.

But this was far from the truth. The new owner, Nick Kovalchick, was himself an enthusiast, and had decided to save the railroad for the enjoyment of those who were old enough to remember and those who were too young to know. Thus, in 1960 the trains were running again, now carrying tourists and railroad fans on a roundtrip excursion from the original depot in Rockhill Furnace, Orbisonia, to the Colgate Grove—a ten-mile ride through the pastoral beauty of the Aughwick Valley.

And today the trains are still running, still looking the same as they always have; the locomotives are a sooty black and the passenger cars an unassuming green. And, still behind the desk he has occupied since 1948, sits Roy Wilburn, operational vice president, supervising activities with an iron hand and a watch which has always shown the correct time.

54

Aging Servants, Still Going Strong

Pictured on the previous page, East Broad Top Rail Road's engine 15 steams back to the Rockhill Furnace depot after having taken on coal and water. Lining the track are rows of rusty hoppers, remnants from the days when the railroad supported itself as a coal carrier. This engine, together with six others—of which four are operational—were bought new from Baldwin between 1911 and 1920. They are all of the 2-8-2 Mikado-type, so called because the first batch to be built by Baldwin was exported to Japan. On this page, above, the venerable engine 15 returns from a roundtrip to Colgate Grove, ducking under a bridge between Shirleysburg and Orbisonia. To the left, the same engine is on its way back to Colgate Grove again, carrying its present-day load of tourists and railroad fans. For the benefit of the photographer, the fireman puts a few additional shovels of coal on the fire, building an extra colorful blaze.

Take a Trip Back in Time

One of the many nostalgic features of the East Broad Top Rail Road, is the now hard-to-find combination of turntable and roundhouse. The structure was built in the classic fan-shape style, using brick and Pennsylvania fieldstone. The years have left it virtually untouched, save for the fact that the original wooden doors have been exchanged for steel doors of the roll-up type. A walk among the old iron horses in the roundhouse—its twilight dusk exaggerated by the huge darkness of the beasts—is truly a trip back in time. Engines 16 and 18, the latter the biggest of the bunch, are both awaiting restoration. The photograph on this page shows engine 15 poised on the turntable. The locomotive weighs 147,000 pounds; the tender adds another 80,000 pounds. With a full load of coal and water, total weight is well over 240,000 pounds. Yet such is the balance built into the turntable that two men, albeit with a bit of effort, are able to turn the engine.

59

Tools of the Trade, and Old Switches

The scene to the left features the oldest type of switch used at East Broad Top, a three-way stub type, used on the side tracks but not out on the main line. A portion of the old shop building forms a fitting backdrop. The shop featured all the necessary machines for proper maintenance of both cars and locomotives. In fact at one time, entire railroad cars were constructed here and in 1927, even a forty-six-ton motor coach was built, propelled by a gasoline engine. Power for the shop itself originally came from a stationary steam engine which operated the various equipment through a system of shafts and belts. The shop stands virtually unchanged today, looking just as it did when the doors closed in the fifties, now only with a decorative layer of dust covering the tools and the workbenches. Pictured above, also unchanged, is the hostler's rack, where all the various cleaning tools still stand at the ready.

WT 70000
6/61 23900

Endangered Bastion of Unplanned Beauty

East Broad Top is paradise for the nostalgia lover. Every change of focus finds yet another time-varnished picture of the past. But how long can it last? Sooner or later the elements will take their toll. When this time comes, can museum-type restoration ever recreate that true, charming patina of unplanned beauty?

63

Splendid Display of Volunteer Spirit

Illinois Railway Museum

In 1957, a group of Chicago railroad enthusiasts decided to stoke the fires in their small organization—founded in 1953—by publishing a newsletter, *Rail & Wire*. The name of the organization itself at this juncture was the Illinois Electric Railway Museum. It counted forty members, and the collection consisted of just six interurban cars, temporarily housed in the North Chicago yard of the Chicago Hardware Foundry.

For the next few years, the members worked diligently, searching for worthy objects to rescue and restore, as well as for a permanent site on which to locate their growing collection. In 1961, the group decided to change its name to the Illinois Railway Museum, an action destined to generate a marked upswing in both interest and activity.

Also that year, the museum was offered a segment of the old Elgin & Belvedere Electric Company right-of-way, running between Huntley and Union, and located seventeen miles north of Elgin. In the spring of 1964, the decision was made to move to this site. And by late summer, forty-two cars had been transferred, and 3,000 feet of rail spiked.

By 1966, work on the track had progressed to the point where the first run could be staged, and an Illinois Terminal interurban car was chosen to perform this task. By the next spring, the museum had acquired a depot, a former Chicago & North Western station house from Marengo, Illinois. In the fall it was time for the first steam operation; the honor was given to engine 5, a 1929 Shay originally used by the Neils Lumber Company. In spite of bad weather and lack of publicity, the first day filled the train with 150 passengers.

Today the museum occupies all of forty-six acres. Three huge barns house the restored collection, and a special steam shed protects the operating locomotives. Altogether, there are more than 225 pieces of equipment, including street cars, elevated rapid transit cars, commuter rapid transit cars, interurban cars, railroad passenger cars, internal combustion locomotives, electric work equipment, railroad work equipment, freight cars and trolley coaches. In addition, there are no less than seventeen locomotives, of which the most imposing is a 2-8-8-2 Norfolk & Western, built by Alco in 1923.

Rail & Wire, now reporting a membership in excess of 500, is still being published, providing a record of this continuing saga of volunteer accomplishment.

The Russian Misses the Revolution

The photograph on the previous page depicts engine 1630—known as the Russian—the main workhorse of the steam department at the Illinois Railway Museum. Parked at the Union depot to rest between runs, the beautifully restored and maintained oldtimer is patiently accepting some well-deserved attention from the fans. In the picture on this spread, the Russian is off and running, at times reaching the impressive speed of 40 mph; track and locomotive condition allow the folks at Union to run at higher speeds than is normally the case on these types of historic operations. The Baldwin was built in 1918 for export to Russia, and was part of a 200-unit batch diverted from shipment at the time of the Russian Revolution. It first went to work on the Frisco line and remained there until the early-fifties, when it was purchased by a Kansas mining company which, when it switched to diesel in the early-sixties, donated the historic locomotive to the museum.

The Magic of Well-oiled Machinery

The photograph on the previous page pictures the Russian while receiving its morning blow-down. Water is drained from the boiler through the blow-off cocks, an operation that flushes out the pollutants, commonly referred to as mud or other unprintable expletives, that have collected at the bottom of the boiler. Thanks to the water being well above boiling temperature, it turns to steam when injected into the air, engulfing the engine in a cloud that always spellbinds the viewer—and the photographer—with its dramatic effect. The Russian boasts a total weight of 230,000 pounds. The overall length is sixty-five feet. The drivers measure fifty-two inches in diameter. The maximum tractive effort is 51,200 pounds, at a boiler pressure of 180 psi. Today, engine 1630 is normally run with around 160 psi of pressure. The photograph on this page pictures a section immediately behind the cylinder where the well-oiled piston rod and the crosshead guides glisten with the sheen of reflected light.

71

Recreating the Golden Age of Railroading

Mid-Continent Railway Museum

Located in Wisconsin's scenic Baraboo hill country, the Mid-Continent Railway Museum has—since its formation in 1959, when just four members kindled the dream—had as its goal to recreate a particular period, one covering the years between 1885 and 1915, the Golden Age of Railroading.

The group gained its first experience in railway operation at Hillsboro, Wisconsin, where a five-mile track had been made available by the Hillsboro & Northeastern Railway. Here the trains were pulled by a locomotive propelled by an internal combustion engine, not one powered by a steam engine, a fact that did not harmonize with the goals of the group.

Still driven by the dream of owning a line that could be operated according to their own ideas, in 1963 the members managed to purchase a weedy right-of-way in North Freedom, four miles long, and a former branch line of Chicago & North Western. The branch was referred to as the Rattlesnake Line, and had been built in 1903 to move iron ore from mines in the La Rue area. When mining operations ceased in 1916, the line stood idle for a year until the track was extended to a quartzite quarry. The quarry closed in 1962, and the line was finally abandoned.

But soon the old embankments were buzzing again. Volunteer railroaders laid new ties, spiked rails and brought in the first restored cars. By June, steam trains were running again, and not just any old steam trains, but ones pulled by a locomotive of the same type that had once operated on the line: an R1-class Ten-Wheeler-type engine built by Alco in 1907 and the former property of Chicago & North Western. Other steam locomotives soon arrived, among them a Mogul-type built by Baldwin in 1884 for the New Orleans & Northeastern Railway. And, from Alberta, Canada, the museum obtained another Ten-Wheeler, built by Montreal in 1913.

Nevertheless, the enthusiasts were not content with recreating the true-to-life atmosphere on the tracks only; it had to be right alongside the track as well. A 1910-style repair shop was erected, and soon the museum was also able to obtain its own depot. This building was originally constructed in 1894 by Chicago & North Western in Rock Springs, located two miles west of North Freedom.

And so the dream of a handful of enthusiasts became reality; a piece of the Golden Age of Railroading has been brought back to life.

Retirement Comes as a Relief

The look of a turn-of-the-century station has been carefully recreated at North Freedom, Wisconsin. In the picture on the previous page, not only the locomotive, but the boxcar in the background, the luggage cart in the foreground loaded with milk cans and the tile on the platform, all collaborate to create the correct atmosphere. The photograph on this page shows the pride of North Freedom, the beautiful 1907 Alco, receiving last-minute attention before steaming out on the line. Originally built for Chicago & North Western, it lived a long and hard life as a freight locomotive in upper Michigan and northern Wisconsin. Even when it was finally taken out of service in 1956, it was not the end of the hard times; the boiler of the old workhorse was subsequently used to thaw ore cars during severe winters. Retired in 1962, it was sold to the museum at scrap value—$2,400.

Locomotive as Art in Motion

Not everyone will agree with the notion that the facade of a steam locomotive can be viewed as a piece of art, but none can deny that it makes an intriguing picture. In this shot, engine 1385 shows off its great drivers—standing sixty-three inches tall—and its massive main and side rods. The geometric pattern of the stay bolts decorate the side of the firebox, and on top of the boiler, silhouetted against the blue sky, the sand and steam domes rise like the humps of a huge camel. Total weight of the sixty-eight-foot-long Alco, including the tender which holds ten tons of coal and 7,500 gallons of water, is 311,500 pounds. Maximum tractive effort is 30,900 pounds at 200 psi of pressure. It is usually kept at around 150 psi now, and the speed at around 20 miles per hour. But speeds in excess of 60 miles per hour are no trouble for this locomotive, the most powerful in the museum's stable, and the last of the 325 Ten-Wheelers built for Chicago & North Western still in operation. The photograph on the following spread shows the old Alco leisurely working out on the line.

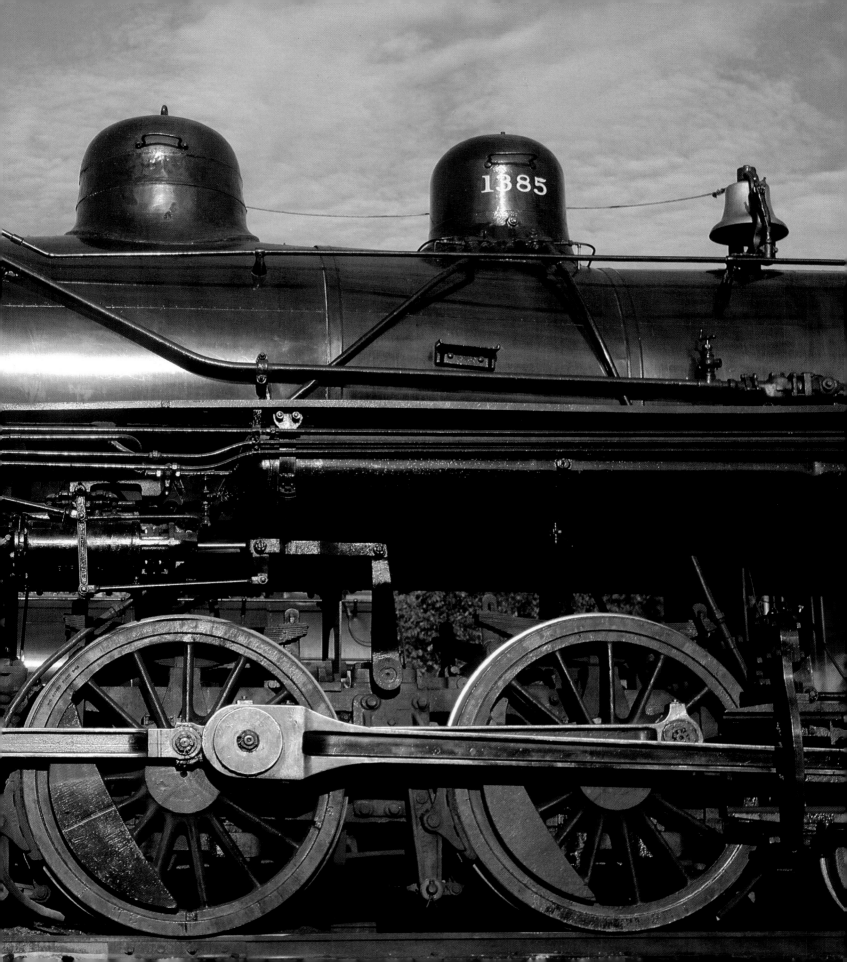

Striking Colors
and Classic Shapes

The earliest roots of the Chicago &
North Western railway, can be
traced back to the Galena &
Chicago Union Railroad, chartered
already in 1836. Another root
system leads back to the Chicago,
St. Paul & Fond du Lac Railroad,
chartered in 1855. By 1859, this
road had been reorganized into the
Chicago & North Western railway.
The merger of the two roads took
place in 1864, and formed the
backbone of the company that over
the years would spread across
Wisconsin, Minnesota, Iowa, South
Dakota and Nebraska, ultimately
reaching as far west as Wyoming.
In the photograph above, the logo of
the Chicago & North Western—
painted on the tender of North
Freedom's Alco—makes a bold
statement, accented against the
background of sooty black and
rows of rivets. Just as dramatic a
background is seen in the picture to
the right with the classic brass bell
projected against a sky of black
smoke.

The Georgetown Loop Lives Again

Georgetown Loop Rail Road

Although it was the 1859 discovery of gold that placed Georgetown on the map, it was the subsequent silver strikes that brought riches to the area. In fact so much silver was hauled out of the Georgetown-Silver Plume district that it became the greatest silver-producing region in the world at the time . . . and riches always attracted the attention of the railroad barons.

A Colorado pioneer, William Loveland, was the first to lay tracks from Denver to Golden—a town he founded—and on toward the west. By 1871, his Colorado Central had tracked six miles into Clear Creek Canyon. Although his immediate aim was to reach the booming mining towns in the region, his ultimate goal was to find a route across the Rockies. The concept of a trans-continental railroad was becoming a reality, and if he could find a way through, Loveland reasoned—thus including Golden on the line—the future of his town would be assured.

Although Loveland indeed found a route, Southern Pacific, builder of the trans-continental railroad, chose to cross in Wyoming instead. Nevertheless, when it came to Loveland's immediate goal—that of reaching Georgetown—railroad tycoon Jay Gould and his Southern Pacific turned out to

be an ally, and as Loveland's funds ran low, Gould stepped in. Thus, in 1877 the railroad finally reached Georgetown.

Now it was a matter of pushing on to Silver Plume, just two miles to the west. But this was easier said than done; the distance presented a rise in elevation of 638 feet, which was too much for any locomotive. The solution was introduced by Robert Blickensderfer, who conceived the idea of a loop that tracked back over itself and thus cut the grade in half. The loop, with its spectacular high-bridge, was completed in 1884.

For a quarter of a century the Georgetown Loop remained a famous tourist attraction, and as such became the nation's first scenic railroad. Referred to in the tourist literature as a Colorado Scenic Wonder, the Loop was probably the most talked-about technical triumph of the railroad era, and was traversed by as many as seven trains per day. But by the twenties, interest declined rapidly, and in the end—which came in 1939—the bridge and the track were scrapped.

It took a group of dedicated railroad enthusiasts, and the Colorado Historical Society, to rebuild the line, including the high-bridge. Thus, in 1984—one hundred years after its birth—the Georgetown Loop was alive again.

Exotic Baldwins
End Up in Colorado

The photograph on the previous page pictures Georgetown's engine 40 as it begins its ascent of the grade leading into the loop. The Consolidation-type 2-8-0 Baldwin and its sister, engine 44, came from El Salvador and Guatemala, where they served with the International Railway of Central America for a number of years. They were both built to burn oil, and still do. The photograph on the following spread captures the train as it traverses the 300-foot-long Devils Gate high-bridge. The span puts the locomotive ninety-six feet above Clear Creek, 8,772 feet above sea level. The bridge was reconstructed by the famous Seabees—the US Navy Reserve Mobile Construction Unit—in 1983, forty-five years after the original had been dismantled and sold for scrap. The photograph on this page features the little Baldwin engine 40—total weight with tender holding 1,400 gallons of fuel and 3,000 gallons of water is 155,000 pounds—at home in the yard at Silver Plume.

Competent Climbers in Close-up

The photographs on this spread focus on Baldwin engine 40 and Georgetown's latest addition, Shay engine 12. The Shay, with its typically offset boiler, is seen to the left. Built in 1927, it came from the West Side Lumber Company in California. Weight is 133,500 pounds, tractive effort 26,000 pounds. For the Baldwin, the comparative figures are 94,000 and 21,000, but the difference in performance is more like the difference between a passenger car and a four-wheel-drive, in favor of the Shay. The photograph above features a close-up of the Baldwin. A plume of steam from the generator exhaust pipe adds a decorative touch.

The High Road to Railroad Heaven

Cumbres & Toltec Scenic Rail Road

No other historic railroad combines natural beauty with authentic atmosphere like the Cumbres & Toltec Scenic Rail Road. Many operations have recreated enchanting environments—admirable efforts by museum-type institutions. Nothing can substitute for the real thing, however. Other railroads feature spectacular scenic beauty—some of equal magnificence—but the allure is diminished by the tourist-attraction fashion in which they operate.

The origin of the Cumbres & Toltec Scenic Rail Road traces back to General William Jackson Palmer, a Pennsylvania railroad engineer and Civil War cavalry officer, whose intention it was to build a north-south line which, starting in Denver, would run to El Paso, cross the Rio Grande and ultimately continue to Mexico City. Hence the name of the company he founded in 1870, the Denver & Rio Grande Railroad.

Palmer began according to plan, building a route to the south and the city of Pueblo. But then he was diverted, turning west— undoubtedly tempted by the riches in the Rocky Mountain mining towns. One spur went up the Arkansas River to Leadville. Another turned off to Aspen and yet another snaked across the Sangre de Cristo range into the San Luis Valley.

Then in 1879, after having sent out survey parties to determine the best route south from his vantage point in the Rockies, Palmer began work on a Silverton extension, which would run from Alamosa down to Antonito, cross the Cumbres Pass, winding in and out across the Colorado and New Mexico borders, reaching heights of 10,000 feet, to Chama, and on to Silverton. The construction crews met with horrible hardships during the winters of 1880 and 1881. But by 1882, the extension was complete and scheduled service could begin.

The trains continued to roll for nearly eighty years. Ore and general freight was hauled, as were passengers and mail. But with the gradual demise of the mining industry, the end was inevitable. The Rio Grande discontinued freight traffic in 1951, but kept limited passenger and excursion-type operation going. When this also ended in 1966, a cry of protest was heard from railroad enthusiasts across the nation. A last-minute decision by the Colorado and New Mexico legislatures, cleared the way for the states to purchase the Antonito to Chama portion, including nine steam engines and 142 pieces of rolling stock. Thus was saved for posterity a chapter of railroad history that could never be rewritten.

A Sight for Sentimental Eyes

Climbing the steep grade toward Cumbres Pass, the Cumbres & Toltec train creates scenes that bring back sentimental memories of a bygone era. On the previous page, engine 484 blows its whistle—mixing white steam with the black smoke—as it closes in on a crossing. The photograph on this spread captures the same unit, moments earlier, passing the old phone booth at Coxo, elevation 9,753 feet. There is still a painful 312 feet to go before the summit at Cumbres Pass is reached. On the following spread, engine 484 is pictured as it is about to leave New Mexico and enter into Colorado. One of Cumbres & Toltec's most illustrious engines, the 484, was a regular on the San Juan, the daily passenger train from Alamosa to Durango. In 1951, it was the helper engine on the last eastbound San Juan, and in 1966, it pulled the last Rio Grande excursion train. Then in 1971, it had the honor of heading Cumbres & Toltec's first revenue train.

92

Trusty Stablemates Since the Twenties

Above, engine 484 breathes out in the Chama yard after a hard day's work. It has just had its supply of coal replenished, and is ready to move on to the engine house. The topped-off pile of coal adds an extra touch of authenticity to the picture on the left. The Cumbres & Toltec runs a team of engines that have been stablemates since the twenties. In 1925, in connection with a general upgrading of its narrow-gauge system, the Rio Grande placed an order for ten

Mikado-type Baldwins. Of these, engines 482, 483, 484, 487, 488 and 489 ended up with Cumbres & Toltec. All are of the same configuration, weighing 286,000 pounds, including the loaded tenders, which hold 9½ tons of coal and 5,000 gallons of water, and produce tractive efforts of 36,500 pounds. On the following spread, a pair of hostlers give engine 489 a once-over before getting down to business. Notice that the outside frame design leaves the driving wheels hidden behind the massive counterweights.

Inside the image, the bulletin board reads:

CHAMA N. M.—TRAIN BULLETI[N]

NO.	DUE	ARRIVE	FROM	FOR	DEP
215		11:10 A	CHAMA	DULCE	11:15
216		4:00 P	DULCE	CHAMA	4:05

DATE 10/12/50

Dark Mysteries and Subtle Messages

The interior of the locomotive cab—with its dark, mysterious crevasses—presents an intriguing photographic challenge. The picture to the right, a time exposure, concentrates on mood rather than detail. Only a few elements manage to attract light. The twin water glasses stand out in the center.

Between them, with its round yellowing face, peers the boiler pressure gauge. From on top of the oil can shelf emerges the squat features of the tallow pot and beside it, the thin beak of the long-spouted oil can. The photograph above, capturing an old bulletin board on the wall inside the Chama depot, conveys messages from the last days of the old Rio Grande railroad.

100

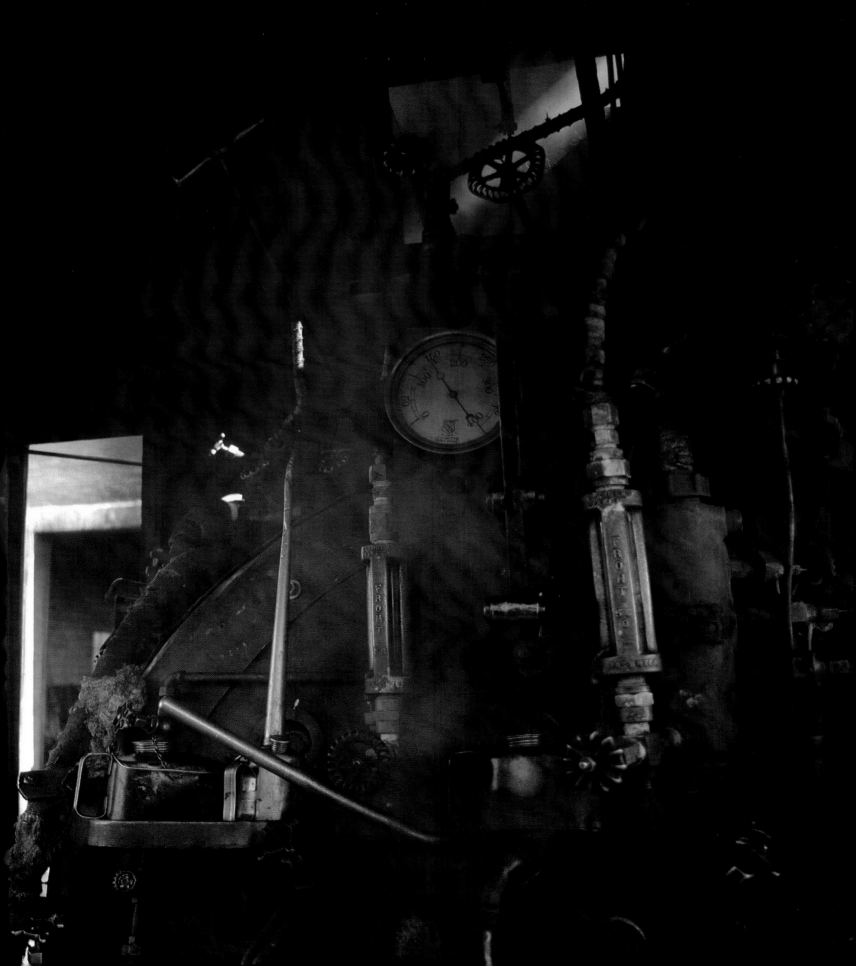

Retracing the Tracks of a Logging Train

Yosemite Mtn & Sugar Pine Rail Road

The Yosemite Mtn & Sugar Pine Rail Road, is a monument to one man's dream—that of Rudy Stauffer. Curiously, the early part of his life was spent in Switzerland, far from the life and times that would so completely capture his fascination. As a child he had heard a visiting pioneer from the Madera Sugar Pine Company, E. C. Wells, tell stories of locomotives hauling enormous logs across the Sierras, and Stauffer had become obsessed by the dream of seeing this with his own eyes.

But by the time Stauffer was able to make the trip in 1954, he found that the logging company had long since closed its doors. Despite this disappointing news, Stauffer decided to settle on the slopes of nearby Yosemite Mountain. On land actually purchased from the same E. C. Wells, Stauffer proceeded to build a small motel, calling it the Swiss Melody Inn. The romantic logging tales were kept alive during walks along the overgrown right-of-way of the abandoned Sugar Pine tracks, which passed right by his prospering motel business.

The Madera Sugar Pine Company had its roots in an 1874 venture by a group of Merced businessmen, who joined capital to build a sawmill in the mountains of northern Fresno County. The novelty of the setup was that the transport of the boards to the San Joaquin Valley would be handled by a fifty-two-mile flume. A local financial panic ended the operation in 1878, but only after the idea had proven to be a sound one.

The Madera Flume & Trading Company took over the business in 1878 and ran it until 1898 when the timber supply was exhausted. The company reorganized the following year, calling itself the Madera Sugar Pine Company, and the milling operation was moved to the location south of Yosemite where it remained until the end in 1933. At the height of its might, the company owned five Shays and an extensive network of track.

In 1965, Stauffer learned that the West Side Lumber Company was looking for a buyer for one of its Shays. Without a firm plan, Stauffer bought the old engine, and proceeded to transport it back to the Swiss Melody Inn. One thing led to another, and soon he obtained the right-of-way, laid track, built observation cars—flatbeds fitted with split logs for the passengers to sit on—and proceeded to run the first train in 1967. Today, the operation has passed on to son Max. A childhood dream realized . . . and passed on to the next generation.

Durable Workers of the Deep Woods

In the photograph on the previous page, engine 15 is seen as it works its way up the grade. The steepest section approaches ten percent. The picture on this spread captures the interior of the engine. Max Stauffer, son of the founder, is at the controls. His right hand holds the throttle lever and the left hand rests on the main brake valve. The long brass lever on the fireman's side controls the firing valve, while the small swivel lever operates the injector valve. The picture on the following spread features the impressive side view of engine 10. It is Sugar Pine's first locomotive, bought by Stauffer in 1965, and also the largest narrow-gauge Shay ever built, weighing a hefty 163,200 pounds. Tractive effort is 36,150 pounds. Engine 15, the latest acquisition, weighs 118,000 pounds and produces 25,830 pounds of tractive effort. In the old logging days, these durable workers operated side by side at the West Side Lumber Company.

104

A Steady Hand and a Sure Eye

Holding the Reins of the Horse

Among the visual experiences that tend to leave deep impressions on the mind, the passing of a train must be counted as a standout. Today, with diesel propulsion having taken over completely, new images can still be gathered, but of course the winners will always remain the ones collected during the era of steam.

The passing of a train always began with that rousing sound of the whistle, distant, drawn out, drawing attention to a billowing cloud of black smoke on the horizon. Soon the locomotive would come into sight. It would seem to move very slowly at first. Then it would come closer, advancing, expanding, finally growing rapidly, looming. And suddenly there would be the rush, that blurred moment, flush with rhythmic throbbing, spinning wheels, bouncing rods and then, afterward, the sweet smell of smoke.

But, whether the passing of the train was observed by a child, riding a bicycle, or by a traveling salesman, stopped in his car at a crossing, or by a farmer in the field, straddling a tractor, the experience would never be complete without a glimpse of the engineer.

The engineer, the man with the cap and the gloves, the man with the goggles, the man in the window, there for a vanishing moment. And often, the man with the wave in response to the wave.

Man was born with an impulse to dominate the beast, be it a wild horse, be it a roaring lion or, in the era of technology, a fast automobile, a screaming airplane . . . or a galloping iron horse. Thus, a child, inspired by the sight of a passing train, would often dream of growing up to become an engineer.

But that was in the old days. Now, there's only a few who know what it's like to run a steam locomotive. And the ones who know are not the ones to talk about it. For how do you describe the relationship with a throttle? That crude lever, demanding such a steady hand. Sometimes one-eighth of an inch is too much. And how do you explain the relationship with a whistle? That mile-wide sound at the extension of your arm. How do you explain the fact that iron can be alive? Alive with sounds. Huffing and puffing. Hissing. Alive with motion. Rocking. Twisting and bending. How do you explain the aloofness behind that quick glance at the boiler pressure? And the preoccupied gaze of a sure eye. And the cool confidence that comes from always knowing what the track looks like behind the next curve.

Proper Gear
Makes the Engineer

Although this statement is an obvious exaggeration—with rhyme seducing reason—it does hold some truth. Years of experience have taught Paul Brock, engineer on Tennessee Valley's engine 630, pictured on the previous page, what he needs to know about clothes that really do the job. The cap is by Kromer. The blue denim shirt has some fancy French name, but the overalls are by Limited. A scarf keeps the cinders out of the neck, and a pair of industrial-type goggles keep them out of the eyes. And completing the picture, at the end of the chain ticks a watch, a 992B Hamilton, sporting twenty-one jewels for accuracy. Pictured above, Brock prepares to take off, reaching for the whistle—two long signals is the proper alert. To the right, Brock has reached operating speed, a maximum of 25 miles per hour on this stretch of track. Approaching a crossing, he again prepares to blow the whistle, one long signal is the proper warning in this instance.

A Measure of Muscle, Brains to Boot

Feeding and Firing the Horse

The fireman must be endowed with an ample collection of muscle, but it isn't the only thing required to make him succeed—he must also be equipped with brains. The reason for this is that every locomotive has its own idiosyncracies, and when it comes to the techniques required to keep the fire going and burning efficiently, the fireman is the one who must figure them out.

So, it's not just a matter of shuffling coal. For instance, a particular locomotive might be equipped with a firebox that produces the most efficient combustion—because of the way it was constructed, or because of the way it has become as a result of age-related changes—when the coal is placed in a string that covers each side of the grate, as well as the area down by the door, thus leaving the center and the front empty.

And efficient combustion is the name of the game. On the relatively short trips taken by most of the tourist-type operations, there can be a difference in fuel consumption at the day's end of half-a-ton of coal between the experienced fireman and the novice. Think then of the difference in cost of operation over a long period of time. No wonder that a fireman with a reputation for knowing how to fire efficiently would be a sought-after professional.

Another item requiring the constant attention of the fireman is the boiler pressure. This is regulated through a combination of manipulating the intensity of the fire in the firebox and the amount of water in the boiler. The water level is controlled by the injector valve, and if the pressure goes too high, water is shut off. If the pressure goes too low, water is added. But as indicated, the pressure is also affected by the fire, and the rule is to add coal before water.

Then there's also the possibility that, if operated with total disregard for these basics, the boiler might blow up. Over the century of steam operation, this has indeed been an unusual occurrence. But photographs do exist showing evidence of the devastating results of such explosions.

The fireman also functions as the eyes of the engineer, who has to contend with a blind spot—well, a blind football-field—on the left side of the locomotive. Thus, when approaching crossings, and during operation in the yard, the fireman keeps an eye out for potential problems.

Does all this sound complicated? Well, it does take more than just muscle.

LOCOMOTIVE
1385

IS OWNED BY

MID CONTINENT RAILWAY
HISTORICAL SOCIETY

NORTH FREEDOM   WISCONSIN

Steel-toed Boots Back in Style

The active nature of the fireman's chores—and the hot environment—combine to keep him warm and constantly on the go. In the photograph on the previous spread, David Mattoon, fireman aboard North Freedom's engine 1385, throws a shovel of nourishment to the hungry iron horse. The butterfly fire door opens automatically, activated pneumatically when the fireman steps on a pedal mounted within convenient reach of his left foot.

Mattoon has been fascinated by locomotives as long as he can remember. A visit to North Freedom when he was ten further cemented this fascination. And in 1978, he began volunteering as a fireman at the Mid-Continent Railway Museum. Posing for the portrait to the left, he still wears the same steel-toed safety boots he wore when starting-out nine years ago. The gloves are of a heavy-duty type worn by welders. Above, Mattoon reaches for yet another load; he figures he moves about 1½ tons of coal on an average day.

A Penchant for Preservation of Iron

Grooming and Greasing the Horse

The word hostler in railroad terminology is a direct transfer of the word as it's used in equestrian parlance. In the early days, there was a natural association between the horses of flesh and blood, and the horses of iron and steel. Thus, the term used to describe the man who cared for the horses also became the term used to describe the man whose profession it was to maintain the locomotives.

During the heyday of the steam locomotive, the total number of individuals employed as professional hostlers must certainly have been counted in the hundreds of thousands. Today the brotherhood of professional hostlers consists of, perhaps, a few dozen. A lost breed indeed.

While the approximately 200 locomotives on active duty today are certainly well cared for, these duties are most often performed by the engineer and the fireman. And since they're usually volunteers, individuals whose sole duty it is to care for the locomotive are only found in the large operations. Even here, the specific area of service performed by hostlers varies.

The Cumbres & Toltec Scenic Rail Road is an example of an operation still run like a railroad of the past. Here, the hostlers arrive when the engineer and the fireman are finished for the day. They take over while the locomotive is still at the head of the train. From there, they move the engine to be resupplied at the water tower, the coal chute and the sand shed.

After these operations are completed, the locomotive is moved to a spot outside the engine house where the running gear and frame is steam-cleaned. The next operation consists of the greasing of the rod bushings. The engine is then moved inside the engine house, placed over the inspection pit and the underside checked for loose or missing parts. At this point, other maintenance as per written instructions from the engineer is performed by separate mechanics. The engine is then tied up for the night.

The next morning, the hostlers prepare the locomotive for the day's duties by, among a host of measures, starting the air pump, cleaning out the ashes, and topping off the water and coal supply. The locomotive is then parked at the head of the train, and the hostlers stay with it until the engineer and the fireman arrive. Thus ends the day, and night, of a hostler. For the few who still do it as a profession, it's a job like other jobs.

Greasing with a Machine Gun

The photograph on the previous spread pictures the daily gathering of the Cumbres & Toltec hostlers. Having punched in at 4:00 in the afternoon, they wait in front of the old station house for the arrival of the 4:30 train. Here, they have just spotted the locomotive. On this page, Ricky Rivas operates the special heavy-duty grease gun, a unique piece of equipment dating back to the days of Rio Grande operation, and working on compressed air. The can hanging from the stand contains pin grease, which comes in blocks approximately the size of a brick. The grease is cut in sticks about ¾ inch wide and six inches long. The hostler, using his left hand, feeds the grease into a tube at the same time as he operates with his right hand an air valve that shoots the grease into the bushings. The use of this machine is a feature exclusive to Cumbres & Toltec; in the case of most other steam operators, the greasing is performed with the help of a hand-operated gun.

119

Digging Up Long-Lost Locomotives

Industrial Archaeology in Action

By what right does a chapter on locomotive derelicts, the dead ones, appear in a book about live steam, the living ones? Well, the most obvious justification is that the dead may some day be brought back to life. And certainly the validity of the argument is underscored by numerous examples of this having happened in the past.

But the most straight-forward reason is that these derelicts simply hold so much intrigue. A book attempting to capture the spirit of live steam would not be complete without it, for in the minds of enthusiasts everywhere is lodged the dream of finding such objects.

A rusty locomotive sitting abandoned, say, in a long-since-closed-down quarry— with its wheels buried in the sand, with restless arms of weeds and brush intertwined with the frozen-up arms of the rods, with flower-filled branches growing through the cab windows, with bees living and raising offspring in the inspection holes of the staybolts—is the land-bound equivalent of a shipwreck on the bottom of the sea.

The shipwreck and the locomotive hold common secrets of a romantic past: there was once life on board, engineers, firemen, passengers; there were once motion and vibration; there were once sounds, of steam, of whistles; and there was the capability of traveling to far-away places.

Railroad folklore is rich with anecdotes of locomotive derelict sightings. One such anecdote tells of a boy and his father, who, after returning from a hunting trip to northern Wisconsin, insisted they had stumbled onto a locomotive, buried deep in the forest, overgrown, hidden among the trees. But the exact location was never revealed, presumably because the explorers wanted to salvage the derelict themselves.

Another such anecdote comes from the high country of Colorado's Rocky Mountains and a small mining town located there. The railroad employed in hauling out the riches ran across steep and treacherous terrain, and, it is said, the bottom of a particular ravine still holds the secrets of rusty locomotives, once having crashed down the hillside, now barely visible, overgrown, impossible to reach and certainly impossible to recover.

Such stories, although perhaps just stories, do justify their existence in the world of industrial archaeology. For sometimes the stories turn out to be true, and a long-lost locomotive can be dug up and brought back to life.

Resting Until Resurrection Day

Pictured on the previous page, the carcass of a huge 0-8-0 Eight-Wheel Switcher-type locomotive. The engine was built in 1929 by Baldwin as part of a twenty-unit requisition from Grand Trunk Western. In the early-fifties, it was sold to North Western Steel and Wire. The intent was to cut it up, but the operators decided to use it for hauling scrap metal instead. The engine is now part of a collection housed at the Illinois Railway Museum. At some point it was converted to burn oil, and this, together with the fact that it has been beaten to death mechanically, makes it an expensive project for restoration. Pictured on this page, Cumbres & Toltec's engine 482 resting in the grass next to the old engine house in Chama. It was retired by the Rio Grande in the late-fifties and sat in the Alamosa yard until it was moved to Chama a few years ago. Used as a source for parts, the engine needs a complete overhaul before it will be able to get back on its wheels again.

The Bright Side
and the Dark Side

The photographs on this spread offer a study in contrasts. To the right, a close-up of the same Cumbres & Toltec engine seen featured on the previous spread. Here the weeds are growing wild, reaching up among the rods, giving an impression of total abandonment. In the picture above,

featuring a close-up of an engine described on the following page, the bright light spotlights a showcase of corrosion, although everything is still there: the rods, the brake hangers, the sand pipes, the springs. At first sight, seen from the dark side, these engines seem to be hopeless basketcases. But not so. All it takes is money and man hours—that's the bright side.

Ravaged by Rust, but Not Written Off

Found in an Illinois gravel pit, this huge Consolidation-type freight locomotive was bought at an auction and towed to the Illinois Railway Museum rolling on its own wheels. The 1916 Baldwin has not been steamed up for thirty years, and has the appalling, and appealing, appearance of a derelict—but what more can you expect for $1,600?